AROHA JOY

THE RETURN OF ALABA

Copyright © 2024 by Aroha Joy

All rights reserved. No part of this publication may be reproduced, stored or transmitted in any form or by any means, electronic, mechanical, photocopying, recording, scanning, or otherwise without written permission from the publisher. It is illegal to copy this book, post it to a website, or distribute it by any other means without permission.

First edition

This book was professionally typeset on Reedsy.
Find out more at reedsy.com

This book is dedicated to God Almighty

Contents

Preface		ii
Acknowledgments		iv
1	The Disappearance	1
2	Shadows of the Past	5
3	The Silent Witness	10
4	The Cabin in the Shadows	15
5	Secrets Unveiled	20
6	The Calm Before the Storm	26
7	Shadows of Doubt	32
8	A Storm on the Horizon	37
9	Shadows of Betrayal	43
10	The Final Stand	48

Preface

I tell the story of Alaba, a young warrior who left his home village years ago, seeking a better life and purpose. The village of Umunze, where Alaba spent his youth, had always been close to his heart, but he had been forced to leave in pursuit of a life beyond the limitations of his humble beginnings. Over the years, he became a skilled fighter, mastering techniques that would eventually lead him to return home, when his village was threatened by a ruthless gang known as the Black Jackals.

I reveal how Alaba's return to Umunze marks the beginning of a new chapter in his life. The once thriving and peaceful village had grown vulnerable to the Black Jackals, a group of merciless raiders led by the cruel Ezenwa. I show the internal struggle Alaba faces as he reconnects with his old village, witnessing the devastation wrought by the gang's violence and realizing how much his absence has affected the villagers. His journey is not just one of physical battles, but emotional and moral ones as well, as he tries to mend his past mistakes while rallying the villagers for their ultimate fight.

I explore Alaba's transformation from a lone fighter into a leader. In the face of overwhelming odds, Alaba inspires the villagers to take up arms and defend their home. I focus on the bond that forms between him and the people who once considered him a stranger. Through their collective determination, they begin to strategize a counterattack, setting the stage for a bloody showdown with the Black Jackals. I emphasize the importance of unity and resilience, showing that the strength of the community can triumph over individual power.

I illustrate the intensity of the conflict as the Black Jackals descend upon the village, intent on claiming it for themselves. I describe the tension as Alaba and his newfound warriors prepare for battle, knowing that they may face annihilation but willing to fight for their survival. The village, despite its modest defenses, stands strong under Alaba's leadership, ready to face the invaders head-on. I also delve into the psychological and emotional stakes of the battle, as Alaba understands that the outcome will define his legacy and the future of Umunze.

I highlight the climactic moment when Alaba faces off against Ezenwa, the leader of the Black Jackals, in a deadly duel. I describe the confrontation in vivid detail, with both men fighting not only for their lives but for everything they believe in. Alaba's victory over Ezenwa marks a turning point in the battle, and the Black Jackals begin to retreat. I make it clear that, although the immediate threat is over, the scars of the battle will remain, and the fight for peace is ongoing.

I show the aftermath of the battle as the villagers, battered but victorious, begin to rebuild their lives. The price of their victory is high, but Alaba knows that they have won more than just the physical war—they have reclaimed their sense of hope and purpose. I end with Alaba's reflection on what it means to return to one's roots and protect what truly matters. Through the events of the battle, Alaba has found a new purpose, not just as a warrior, but as a protector of his people.

Acknowledgments

Thank you for your love and support

1

The Disappearance

The morning was like any other in Okeji, a quiet village nestled between rolling hills and thick forests. The air carried the aroma of freshly tilled earth as farmers prepared their fields for planting. Children dashed around the village square, their laughter echoing in the crisp air. Life in Okeji thrived in its usual rhythm—until Alaba vanished.

Alaba was not just any man in Okeji. He was a pillar of the community, a voice of wisdom, and a symbol of hope. A tall, broad-shouldered man in his late thirties, he had a way of drawing people in with his warm smile and calm demeanor. His laughter was a balm for the soul, his counsel a guide for the troubled. To many, Alaba was the kind of man whose presence alone could keep a community united.

That morning, Alaba was seen walking towards the forest with his leather satchel slung over his shoulder. A few villagers waved at him, and he waved back, his smile as reassuring as ever. It was not unusual for Alaba to wander into the forest. He often went there to gather herbs or reflect in solitude. But this time was different.

Hours turned into an entire day, and Alaba did not return. At first, the villagers dismissed it as nothing out of the ordinary. "Perhaps he decided to visit the next village," one elder speculated. But when the second day dawned and there was still no sign of him, concern began to ripple through the community like an unspoken curse.

Adaeze, Alaba's wife, was the first to sense that something was terribly wrong. She stood at the edge of the forest, her eyes scanning the dense foliage as though willing him to emerge. Her heart pounded in her chest as she clutched her baby boy close. "Alaba would never stay away like this," she murmured, more to herself than to the small crowd gathering behind her.

"He didn't say anything to you about going somewhere far?" asked Ojiugo, the village seamstress, her face creased with worry.

Adaeze shook her head, tears glistening in her eyes. "No. He left after breakfast, saying he'd be back before noon. Something isn't right."

The village elder, Pa Eze, raised his staff, signaling for silence. His frail frame belied the authority in his voice as he addressed the crowd. "We cannot assume the worst yet," he began, his voice steady despite the growing tension. "We will form search parties. Let no corner of the forest be left unchecked."

Within the hour, groups of men and women armed with machetes and torches spread out into the forest. They called Alaba's name, their voices breaking through the chirping of birds and rustling leaves. Every rustle of the underbrush made their hearts leap, but the forest offered no answers, only an eerie silence that grew heavier with each passing hour.

As the sun dipped below the horizon, the search parties returned empty-handed. Adaeze's face crumpled in despair as she sank to her knees. "Where could he be?" she whispered, clutching her son tightly.

Theories about Alaba's disappearance began to swirl through the village. Some suggested he might have been attacked by wild animals, though no signs of a struggle had been found. Others whispered about forest spirits known to abduct wandering souls. Then there were those who believed Alaba had simply abandoned his family—a notion that Adaeze vehemently rejected.

"Alaba would never do such a thing," she insisted to anyone who dared voice such thoughts. "He loved this village. He loved us. Something has happened to him."

The turning point came on the third day when young Ebuka, a boy known for his sharp eyes and quick feet, stumbled upon a clue. Near a stream deep in the forest, he found Alaba's satchel, its contents scattered on the ground. There was no blood, no sign of a struggle—just the satchel and its spilled contents: a journal, a few herbs, and a half-eaten loaf of bread.

Ebuka ran back to the village, breathless as he waved the satchel in the air. "I found this!" he cried. The villagers gathered around, examining the items as though they could unravel the mystery.

Pa Eze's brow furrowed as he inspected the journal. "These are Alaba's writings," he said. "But why would he leave his satchel behind?"

The discovery only deepened the mystery. That night, the village square was alive with hushed conversations. Theories turned darker—some spoke of a stranger who had been seen talking to Alaba days before his disappearance. This man, they said, was not from Okeji and had asked peculiar questions about the forest.

"I remember him," said Nneka, the village weaver. "He came to my stall asking about herbs. He didn't seem dangerous, but now... I wonder."

The villagers resolved to find this stranger, though no one knew his name or where he had gone. Meanwhile, Adaeze prayed fervently in the small hut she shared with her children. Her voice cracked with emotion as she called out to the heavens. "Bring my husband back to me," she pleaded.

By the end of the week, the mood in Okeji had shifted from concern to fear. The forest, once a source of life and sustenance, now seemed ominous and unwelcoming. And as the villagers lit their lanterns each night, they wondered what fate had befallen Alaba and whether they would ever see him again.

Unbeknownst to them, deep within the forest, shadows moved. Alaba's story was far from over—it was only just beginning.

2

Shadows of the Past

The days following Alaba's disappearance passed in a haze of confusion and sorrow. The once-vibrant village of Okeji was shrouded in an air of despondency, as though its very soul had been stolen. Children no longer laughed in the streets, and the elders, who once sat under the baobab tree exchanging tales of old, grew silent and withdrawn.

For Adaeze, life became a blur of restless nights and relentless worry. She could barely eat or sleep, her mind consumed by thoughts of her husband. Clutching the satchel that had been found in the forest, she poured over its contents in the quiet hours of the night, searching for any clue to his whereabouts. The journal inside, filled with Alaba's tidy handwriting, became her lifeline.

In one of the entries, written just days before his disappearance, Alaba had scrawled a cryptic message:

"The past always finds a way to return. I fear it may soon catch up with me. If anything happens, Adaeze, know that I love you and the children more than life itself."

Adaeze's hands trembled as she read the words. What past was Alaba referring to? She had known him for years, and though he rarely spoke about his life before coming to Okeji, she had assumed it was unremarkable. Yet the tone of this entry suggested otherwise.

Determined to uncover the truth, Adaeze turned to Pa Eze. The elder had always been close to Alaba, treating him like a son. If anyone knew what Alaba's words meant, it would be him.

"Pa Eze," she said one evening, her voice heavy with desperation, "what do you know about Alaba's life before he came to this village? He wrote something in his journal... something about his past catching up with him."

The old man sighed, his face etched with sorrow. "It is not my story to tell, Adaeze," he began, but when he saw the pain in her eyes, he relented. "But perhaps it is time you knew."

Pa Eze motioned for her to sit beside him under the baobab tree. The sun was setting, casting long shadows across the village. He began his tale, his voice low and measured.

"Alaba was not always the man you know. Before he came to Okeji, he lived in the bustling city of Lagos. He was young, ambitious, and... reckless. Like many others, he dreamed of wealth and status, but the path he chose was not an honest one. Alaba became involved with a group of men—dangerous men—who operated on the fringes of society. They called themselves *The Black Jackals*."

Adaeze gasped. "The Black Jackals? The same gang that was in the news for smuggling and robbery?"

Pa Eze nodded gravely. "The very same. Alaba never told me the full extent of his involvement, but he admitted that he did things he wasn't proud of. He said he joined them out of desperation, but as time went on, he realized the cost was too great. He tried to leave, but leaving the Jackals is not easy. It is a group bound by blood oaths and threats of violence."

"What happened?" Adaeze asked, her voice barely above a whisper.

"Alaba fled," Pa Eze continued. "He left Lagos under the cover of night and came here, to Okeji, hoping to start a new life. He told me he had severed all ties with his past, but he was always afraid it would catch up with him. That is why he never shared these details with anyone else—not even you."

Adaeze felt a mix of emotions: shock, fear, and a deep sadness for the man she loved. She now understood why Alaba had been so private about his past, but the knowledge brought her no comfort. If the Black Jackals had found him, his life could be in grave danger.

"Do you think they've come for him?" she asked.

Pa Eze hesitated. "It is possible. But we cannot jump to conclusions. We need more information."

That night, Adaeze decided to act. She sought out Nneka, the weaver who had mentioned the stranger seen speaking to Alaba days before his disappearance.

"Nneka," she began, "please, tell me everything you remember about the man who spoke to my husband."

Nneka frowned, her hands pausing over the loom. "I didn't think much of it at the time," she admitted. "He came to my stall asking about herbs and the forest. He had a strange air about him—polite, but guarded. I saw him talking to Alaba later that day. They seemed to be arguing."

"What did he look like?"

"He was tall, with a scar across his left cheek. He wore a red cap and carried a walking stick. That's all I remember."

Adaeze's heart sank. She had no idea who this man was, but his description sounded menacing. Could he have been a member of the Black Jackals, sent to track down Alaba?

The next day, Adaeze shared what she had learned with Pa Eze and a small group of trusted villagers. They decided to search the forest again, this time focusing on the area near the stream where Alaba's satchel had been found.

As the group ventured into the dense foliage, Adaeze's mind raced. Memories of her life with Alaba flooded her thoughts—his laughter as he played with their children, the way he always kissed her forehead before leaving the house, his dreams of building a better future for their family. She couldn't lose him now, not when they had so much left to share.

Hours into the search, the group stumbled upon something chilling: a makeshift campsite, abandoned but recently used. The ashes of a fire still smoldered, and scattered around were food wrappers and footprints leading deeper into the forest.

"Someone was here," said Chike, one of the villagers. "And not long ago."

Adaeze's heart pounded. Was this where Alaba had been taken? Or had the stranger been hiding here, waiting for the right moment to strike?

The group pressed on, following the footprints as they twisted through the dense underbrush. With every step, Adaeze felt a growing sense of dread. The shadows of Alaba's past were no longer just stories—they were real, and they were closing in.

As the sun dipped below the horizon, the group reached a clearing. There, carved into the trunk of a tree, was a single symbol: a black jackal.

Adaeze's blood ran cold. Alaba's past had returned, and it was far darker than she had imagined.

3

The Silent Witness

The sight of the black jackal carved into the tree struck Adaeze like a blow. She stumbled backward, her breath coming in short gasps. The symbol was unmistakable—a sinister reminder that Alaba's past had found him. The villagers, too, stood frozen, staring at the carving as if it might spring to life and attack.

Chike was the first to break the silence. "This confirms it," he said, his voice grim. "The Black Jackals are involved. They've been here."

"But why?" Adaeze whispered. "Why now, after all these years?"

Pa Eze placed a reassuring hand on her shoulder. "Whatever their reasons, we must tread carefully. If they've taken Alaba, it means they want something from him. But it also means he may still be alive."

The thought gave Adaeze a glimmer of hope, though it was tempered by fear. The Black Jackals were not known for mercy. She had heard stories of their ruthlessness, how they left no loose ends. If they had captured Alaba, it was likely for reasons far darker than she dared imagine.

The group decided to return to the village to regroup and plan their next steps.

As they made their way back, Adaeze couldn't shake the feeling that they were being watched. The forest, usually teeming with life, felt unnervingly quiet. Every crackle of a twig underfoot made her jump.

By the time they reached the village, it was nearly dark. Adaeze immediately went to her hut, her mind racing. She knew they had little time. If the Black Jackals had come for Alaba, they wouldn't stay long. She needed answers—fast.

That night, as the village settled into an uneasy sleep, Adaeze sat alone by the dim glow of a lantern. She opened Alaba's journal again, combing through its pages for any hint of what might have led the Jackals to him. Most of the entries were mundane—notes about farming, observations about village life, and musings on his love for his family. But one entry caught her eye:

"I've heard whispers of movement in the city. The Jackals are looking for something—or someone. If they find out where I am, it could mean trouble. I've lived in peace for too long to let them destroy it now. I must prepare."

Adaeze's chest tightened. Alaba had known they were coming. But what were they looking for? And why had he kept this from her?

Unable to sleep, she decided to seek out Pa Eze again. She found him sitting outside his hut, staring at the stars.

"You're restless," he said as she approached.

"I can't stop thinking about what Alaba wrote," she admitted, handing him the journal. "He knew they were coming. He must have been hiding something."

Pa Eze read the entry silently, his brow furrowing. When he finished, he sighed heavily. "There's more to this than we know," he said. "Alaba was a good man, but even good men carry secrets. If he believed the Jackals were after him, it means he might have taken something from them—or known something they wanted to keep buried."

"What could he have taken?" Adaeze asked, her voice tinged with frustration. "He left everything behind when he came to Okeji."

"Maybe not everything," Pa Eze replied. "Sometimes, the things we carry aren't physical. They're memories, knowledge, or promises we've made."

His words unsettled Adaeze. If Alaba had been hiding something all these years, what could it be? And why would the Jackals go to such lengths to find him now?

The next morning, a breakthrough came from an unexpected source. Young Ebuka, the boy who had found Alaba's satchel, approached Adaeze as she prepared breakfast for her children.

"Auntie Adaeze," he said, tugging at her wrapper, "I saw something in the forest yesterday, but I was too scared to tell anyone."

Adaeze knelt to his level, her heart pounding. "What did you see, Ebuka?"

"There was a man," the boy whispered, glancing around nervously. "He was hiding behind a tree near the clearing. He didn't see me, but I saw him. He had a red cap and a scar on his face."

Adaeze's blood ran cold. The stranger Nneka had described.

"Did you hear him say anything?" she asked, her voice trembling.

Ebuka nodded. "He was talking to someone. I couldn't see who, but he said, 'We don't have much time. The others are getting impatient.'"

Adaeze's stomach churned. The stranger wasn't alone, and they were planning something.

"Thank you, Ebuka," she said, forcing a smile despite her growing fear. "You were very brave to tell me."

She wasted no time relaying the information to Pa Eze and the search party. "We need to act now," she urged. "They're still in the forest, and they're planning something. If we wait any longer, we might lose our chance to find Alaba."

Pa Eze nodded, his expression grave. "You're right. We'll gather the men and set out at once."

By midday, a larger group of villagers armed with machetes, bows, and arrows set off into the forest. Adaeze insisted on joining them, despite protests from the others.

"This is my husband," she said firmly. "I won't stay behind while his life is at stake."

The group moved cautiously, following Ebuka's directions to the clearing. The closer they got, the more tense the atmosphere became. Adaeze could feel the weight of every step, her heart pounding in her chest.

When they reached the clearing, it was empty. The campsite was gone, and the footprints had been obscured. But as they searched the area, Chike found something hidden in the underbrush: a strip of fabric torn from a shirt.

Adaeze recognized it instantly. "This is Alaba's," she said, clutching the fabric tightly.

The discovery reignited their determination. They pressed on, deeper into the forest, until they came upon something unexpected—a small, dilapidated cabin hidden among the trees. Smoke rose from its chimney, and the faint sound of voices could be heard inside.

Pa Eze signaled for the group to stop. "We've found them," he whispered.

Adaeze's heart raced. Alaba was close. But so was danger, lurking behind that cabin door.

4

The Cabin in the Shadows

The sight of the cabin sent a shiver down Adaeze's spine. It was a forgotten relic, weathered by time, with vines creeping along its walls. The air around it felt thick with tension, as if the forest itself held its breath. The faint sound of voices coming from inside confirmed their worst fears: whoever had taken Alaba was here.

Pa Eze raised his hand to signal the group to spread out. "We'll surround the cabin," he whispered. "No sudden moves. We need to know what we're up against."

Adaeze clutched the piece of Alaba's torn shirt as if it were a lifeline. She had insisted on joining the search, but now that they were here, the weight of what they might find threatened to overwhelm her. She steeled herself. If Alaba was inside, she had to be strong.

The villagers crept forward silently, their weapons ready. Chike led a small group toward the cabin's rear, while Pa Eze and Adaeze stayed near the front. Adaeze's eyes scanned the clearing for any sign of movement. The voices inside grew louder, though the words were muffled.

Pa Eze leaned closer to Adaeze. "Stay back," he urged.

"No," she whispered fiercely. "I have to see this through."

Before Pa Eze could argue, a loud crash from inside the cabin shattered the tense silence. The voices erupted into shouts, and the door burst open.

Two men emerged, both armed with knives. One was tall and wiry, with a scar running down his cheek. The other was shorter, his face partially obscured by a red cap. Their eyes widened as they saw the villagers, but the shock quickly turned to defiance.

"Who are you?" the scarred man barked, his knife glinting in the sunlight.

"We could ask you the same," Pa Eze replied calmly, stepping forward. His tone was steady, but his grip on his machete was firm. "This is our land. You have no business here."

The shorter man chuckled darkly. "Your land, old man? Do you even know who you're dealing with?"

Adaeze stepped forward before Pa Eze could stop her. "Where is my husband?" she demanded, her voice shaking with anger and fear. "Where is Alaba?"

The mention of Alaba's name seemed to startle the men. They exchanged a glance, their bravado faltering for a moment.

The scarred man sneered. "So you're his woman. I'd say it's a shame, but your husband brought this on himself."

"What do you mean?" Adaeze pressed, her heart pounding. "What did he do?"

The shorter man stepped closer, his knife still raised. "Alaba thought he could outrun his past. But the Black Jackals never forget. He owes us, and we always collect."

Adaeze felt her stomach drop. The Black Jackals. The name alone was enough to make anyone tremble. She had heard whispers of their cruelty, their ironclad grip on those who crossed them. But hearing it confirmed sent chills through her.

"What does he owe you?" she asked, trying to keep her voice steady.

The scarred man smirked. "That's none of your concern. All you need to know is that he's paying his debt, one way or another."

Before anyone could react, Chike and his group emerged from the back of the cabin, weapons drawn. The two men were now surrounded.

"Where is Alaba?" Chike demanded, his voice like steel.

The shorter man raised his hands in mock surrender. "He's alive, for now," he said. "But if you think you can take him back, you're more foolish than I thought."

"We'll see about that," Chike growled.

The tension reached a breaking point as the villagers closed in. The scarred man lunged suddenly, slashing at Pa Eze. The elder stepped back just in time, swinging his machete to block the attack. The clearing erupted into chaos as the villagers fought to subdue the intruders.

Adaeze stayed back, her heart racing. She wanted to help, but fear rooted her in place. She watched as Chike and another villager wrestled the shorter man to the ground, disarming him. The scarred man, however, was proving to be a formidable opponent, dodging strikes and landing blows with alarming precision.

Finally, Pa Eze managed to land a decisive hit, striking the scarred man's arm and forcing him to drop his knife. The villagers quickly restrained both men, tying their hands with rope.

"Where is Alaba?" Pa Eze demanded, his voice cold.

The scarred man spat on the ground. "You think you've won? You have no idea what's coming."

Chike grabbed the man by his collar. "Talk, or we'll make you wish you had."

The man hesitated, his eyes darting between the villagers. Finally, he muttered, "He's in the cabin. But you're too late. The others will be back soon, and when they come, none of you will leave this forest alive."

Ignoring the threat, Adaeze ran toward the cabin, her heart in her throat. Pa Eze and Chike followed closely behind.

Inside, the air was thick and musty, the dim light revealing a room in disarray. At first, Adaeze saw nothing but overturned furniture and scattered belongings. Then, in the corner, she spotted him.

"Alaba!" she cried, rushing to his side.

He was bound and gagged, his face bruised and swollen. His eyes widened as he saw her, tears streaming down his face. Adaeze quickly untied him, pulling him into her arms.

"I thought I'd lost you," she whispered, her voice breaking.

Alaba winced as he tried to speak. "Adaeze... you shouldn't have come. It's not safe."

"We'll talk later," Pa Eze said, helping Alaba to his feet. "Right now, we need to get out of here before the others return."

As they emerged from the cabin, the villagers formed a protective circle around Alaba. The scarred man and his accomplice were still restrained, but their smug expressions suggested they knew something the villagers didn't.

"You can't run from them," the scarred man called out as the group began to retreat. "The Black Jackals will find you. And when they do, you'll wish you had stayed hidden."

Adaeze ignored him, focusing on Alaba. He was alive, but the danger was far from over. The forest seemed darker now, the trees looming like silent witnesses to their peril.

As they made their way back to the village, Adaeze couldn't shake the feeling that their fight was only beginning. Whatever Alaba's past with the Black Jackals, it was clear they weren't going to let him go without a final reckoning.

5

Secrets Unveiled

The villagers carried Alaba back through the forest, their steps quick and deliberate. Although they had rescued him, a heavy silence hung over the group. The scarred man's words echoed in Adaeze's mind: *"You can't run from them."*

When they reached the village, the gathering crowd erupted in relief and curiosity. Alaba was alive but battered, and questions swirled like the wind. Pa Eze raised a hand to quiet everyone.

"We've brought Alaba back," he said, his voice firm. "But trouble follows. Everyone must stay vigilant. The men who attacked him belong to a dangerous group, and they may come here looking for him."

Whispers rippled through the crowd. The mention of a "dangerous group" unsettled them. Adaeze stayed by Alaba's side as they guided him to their home. He leaned on her heavily, his steps faltering.

"Thank you," he murmured, his voice hoarse.

"We'll talk inside," Adaeze replied softly, her heart aching at the sight of his injuries.

—-

In their small hut, Alaba sat down slowly on a wooden stool. His hands trembled as Adaeze cleaned the cuts on his face. She worked in silence, but her thoughts churned with questions.

When she finally spoke, her voice was quiet but firm. "What did they mean, Alaba? What debt do you owe them?"

Alaba's shoulders tensed. He avoided her gaze, staring at the floor as if it might swallow him whole.

"Alaba," she pressed. "You can't keep this from me anymore. These men nearly killed you. They threatened our village. I deserve to know the truth."

He let out a shaky breath. "It's not that simple, Adaeze. If I tell you, everything will change."

"Everything has *already* changed!" she snapped, her voice breaking. "Look at you! Look at what they've done! Do you think they'll stop now? Do you think they'll just walk away?"

Alaba finally looked at her, his eyes filled with guilt and pain. "You're right," he admitted. "You deserve to know."

He paused, gathering his thoughts, before beginning.

—-

"Years ago, before I came to this village, I was a different man. I was reckless, chasing after easy money and cheap thrills. That's when I met the Black Jackals."

Adaeze's breath caught. The name alone sent chills through her.

"They're not just a gang," Alaba continued. "They're an empire. Smuggling, extortion, theft — they thrive on fear and violence. And back then, I was desperate enough to join them. I thought it would be easy money, just a way to survive. But once you're in, there's no getting out."

He clenched his fists, his knuckles white. "At first, it was small jobs. Delivering packages, running errands. But then they started demanding more. They wanted loyalty, absolute loyalty. And if you didn't comply..."

His voice trailed off, but the unspoken words hung heavy in the air.

"I couldn't take it anymore," he said after a moment. "I wanted out. I thought if I disappeared, changed my name, started over, they'd forget about me. That's why I came here. I thought I was safe."

Adaeze's mind raced. She had known Alaba for years, had built a life with him. And yet this part of his past had been hidden from her.

"Why now?" she asked. "Why are they after you again?"

"I don't know," he admitted, his voice filled with frustration. "Maybe they never stopped looking. Maybe I crossed paths with someone who recognized me. But now they've found me, and they won't stop until they get what they want."

"What *do* they want?"

Alaba's face darkened. "Money. Revenge. Control. Once you owe them, they own you. And even if I gave them everything I have, it wouldn't be enough."

Adaeze sat back, her mind spinning. This was more than she had ever imagined.

The Black Jackals weren't just Alaba's problem — they were now hers, and the entire village's.

—-

That evening, Pa Eze and Chike came to the hut. Adaeze had sent word that Alaba was ready to speak, and the two men entered with grave expressions.

"You've put us all in danger," Pa Eze said bluntly, his eyes boring into Alaba. "We need to know exactly what we're dealing with."

Alaba nodded, recounting his story once more. Pa Eze listened intently, his face growing more somber with each detail.

"These men won't stop," Chike said when Alaba finished. "We need to prepare. If they come here, we have to defend ourselves."

Pa Eze sighed. "The villagers must be warned. But we can't panic them. We need a plan."

"What about the men we captured?" Adaeze asked. "They might know more."

"They're being guarded," Chike replied. "But they haven't said much. Just more threats."

"Then we need to make them talk," Adaeze said, her voice firm. "If they know when the others are coming, we need that information."

Pa Eze nodded slowly. "I'll handle it. But Alaba, if there's anything else you haven't told us, now is the time."

Alaba shook his head. "I've told you everything I know. But you're right — they won't stop. Not until I'm dead or they've destroyed everything I care about."

— -

The next day, the village was on high alert. Pa Eze called a meeting in the central square, where he addressed the villagers with measured urgency.

"We face a grave threat," he began. "A group of dangerous men may come here. We don't know when, but we must be ready. Everyone will have a role to play in defending our home."

The villagers murmured among themselves, fear and determination mingling in their expressions.

"We'll need to set up patrols," Chike added. "Fortify the village. And most importantly, stay united. If we stand together, we can face whatever comes."

As plans were made, Adaeze stayed close to Alaba. Despite his injuries, he insisted on helping, though the villagers regarded him with a mix of sympathy and suspicion.

Later that evening, Pa Eze returned with news.

"The men we captured finally talked," he said. "The Black Jackals are planning to come in three days. They're bringing reinforcements."

Three days. The words sent a ripple of dread through Adaeze. It wasn't much time, but it was enough to prepare — if they worked together.

— -

As the sun set, casting a golden glow over the village, Adaeze and Alaba sat outside their hut. The air was cool and still, a fragile peace before the storm.

"I'm sorry," Alaba said quietly, breaking the silence.

"For what?" Adaeze asked, though she already knew.

"For bringing this to you. To the village. You deserve better than this."

Adaeze took his hand, her grip firm. "We've faced challenges before, Alaba. We'll face this one too. Together."

Her words gave him a glimmer of hope. For the first time in days, he allowed himself to believe that they might survive this.

But as the night deepened, Adaeze couldn't shake the feeling that the worst was yet to come.

In three days, the Black Jackals would arrive. And when they did, everything would be decided — their survival, their future, and whether the secrets of Alaba's past would finally be laid to rest.

6

The Calm Before the Storm

The days leading up to the Black Jackals' arrival were tense, each hour marked by a flurry of activity. The village transformed into a makeshift fortress, with barricades erected at key points and patrols stationed around the perimeter. The once serene community now bristled with unease, the air thick with anticipation.

Adaeze worked tirelessly, rallying the women to prepare food and stockpile water while the men trained with Chike in basic defense techniques. Even the children were tasked with carrying messages and gathering stones to use as weapons. No one was spared the weight of the impending danger.

Alaba, despite his injuries, refused to stay idle. He helped reinforce the barricades, his hands raw and blistered from the effort. The villagers still regarded him with caution, but as he threw himself into the preparations, some began to see his sincerity.

Pa Eze, however, remained skeptical. He watched Alaba closely, his gaze sharp and probing.

"Alaba," he said one evening, pulling him aside. "There's something I need to know. If these men come for you, will they stop with you? Or will they destroy this village regardless?"

Alaba hesitated, his jaw tightening. "They'll do whatever it takes to send a message. But if they get me, they might leave the rest of you alone."

Pa Eze's expression darkened. "And if they don't?"

"Then we fight," Alaba said firmly. "We fight to protect what we've built here."

—-

That night, Adaeze found Alaba sitting alone by the fire, his shoulders slumped with exhaustion. She approached him silently, placing a hand on his arm.

"You should rest," she said gently.

"I can't," he replied, his voice heavy. "Every time I close my eyes, I see them. The things they did, the things I did. I can't escape it."

"You've already taken the first step," she said. "You've faced your past. Now it's about protecting your future."

Alaba looked at her, his eyes filled with gratitude and sorrow. "You deserve better than this, Adaeze. Better than me."

"Stop saying that," she said, her voice firm. "We're in this together, Alaba. No matter what happens."

He reached for her hand, holding it tightly. In that moment, the weight of their shared struggle felt a little lighter.

—-

The following morning, Pa Eze called another meeting in the square. The villagers gathered, their faces tense but resolute.

"We've done all we can to prepare," he said. "But we must also have a plan if the worst happens. Women and children will take shelter in the old granary. The rest of us will defend the village."

Adaeze stepped forward. "I want to fight," she said, her voice steady.

Pa Eze frowned. "Your place is with the others, Adaeze. You'll be safer there."

"No one is safe," she countered. "And I can't stand by while the people I love risk their lives."

A murmur of agreement rippled through the crowd. Pa Eze studied her for a long moment before nodding.

"Very well," he said. "But you'll stay near the barricades, where it's safer."

Adaeze nodded, her heart pounding. She wasn't sure if she was ready, but she knew she had to try.

—-

As the sun dipped below the horizon, the village settled into an uneasy stillness. The final preparations were made, and the villagers gathered around small fires, sharing quiet moments of camaraderie.

Alaba and Adaeze sat with Chike and Pa Eze, the flickering flames casting shadows across their faces.

"What if they don't come?" Adaeze asked softly, voicing the question on everyone's mind.

"They'll come," Alaba said with certainty. "The Jackals never make empty threats."

Chike nodded. "Then we'll be ready. They may have numbers, but we have something stronger — a reason to fight."

Pa Eze raised a hand, signaling for silence. "We've done all we can. Now, we wait. Whatever happens tomorrow, we face it together."

—-

The dawn of the third day brought an eerie calm. The village was quiet, the usual bustle replaced by tense anticipation. The barricades were manned, and the patrols were doubled. Even the air felt heavier, charged with the promise of conflict.

Adaeze stood by the main barricade, her heart racing as she scanned the horizon. Alaba was nearby, his posture rigid, his eyes fixed on the forest.

Then, in the distance, a sound broke the silence — the faint thud of drums.

"They're coming," Chike said grimly, his hand tightening around the spear he carried.

The villagers braced themselves as the sound grew louder, accompanied by the low hum of voices. Shadows appeared among the trees, resolving into the shapes of men.

The Black Jackals had arrived.

—-

The attackers emerged from the forest, a motley crew of hardened men armed with machetes, clubs, and crude firearms. Their leader, a tall man with a scar running down his face, stepped forward. His gaze swept over the barricades, a smirk tugging at his lips.

"Alaba!" he called out, his voice carrying across the clearing. "You've caused us a lot of trouble, old friend. It's time to settle your debt."

Alaba stepped forward, his hands clenched into fists. "This ends here," he said, his voice steady despite the fear coursing through him. "You'll get nothing from me or this village."

The leader laughed, a harsh sound that echoed through the trees. "Brave words for a dead man."

He raised a hand, and his men surged forward.

—-

The battle that followed was chaotic and brutal. The villagers fought with everything they had, using spears, stones, and sheer determination to hold the attackers at bay.

Adaeze found herself in the thick of it, her heart pounding as she swung a makeshift club at an advancing Jackal. The man fell, but another took his place almost immediately.

Alaba fought with a ferocity born of desperation. He faced the leader head-on, their weapons clashing as they circled each other.

"You should have stayed gone," the leader sneered, slashing at Alaba.

"And let you destroy everything I care about?" Alaba countered, dodging the blow.

Their fight was brutal, neither man giving an inch. Around them, the villagers and Jackals clashed, the air filled with shouts and the clang of weapons.

—-

By the time the sun set, the battle was over. The Jackals had been driven back, but the cost was high. Several villagers lay wounded, and the square was littered with the debris of the fight.

Alaba stood amidst the wreckage, his chest heaving. The leader of the Jackals lay at his feet, unconscious but alive.

"We've won," Chike said, his voice weary but triumphant.

Pa Eze nodded, his expression somber. "But this isn't the end. The Jackals will come back. We need to be ready."

As the villagers began to tend to the wounded and rebuild, Adaeze approached Alaba.

"You did it," she said, her voice filled with relief.

"We all did," he replied, his eyes meeting hers.

For now, the village was safe. But the battle had left scars, and the shadow of the Black Jackals loomed large. The fight for their future was far from over.

7

Shadows of Doubt

The village bore the scars of battle. Broken fences, shattered tools, and bloodstained ground were stark reminders of the violence that had unfolded. Yet, amidst the ruins, life persisted. Women carried pots of water to douse the fires that still smoldered, men worked to repair the barricades, and children picked up scattered belongings, their wide eyes betraying their lingering fear.

Alaba stood in the center of the village square, surveying the scene. His body ached from the fight, his muscles stiff and bruised, but it was the weight in his heart that dragged him down. For every villager who now looked at him with newfound respect, there were others who still viewed him with suspicion.

"You saved us," Adaeze had told him the night before, her voice filled with gratitude. Yet even her words couldn't erase the memory of Pa Eze's wary eyes.

—-

The morning after the battle, the village gathered for a meeting. Pa Eze stood at the front, his hands clasped tightly behind his back. His posture was rigid, his face drawn.

"We survived," he began, his voice carrying over the murmurs of the crowd. "But this is not the end. The Black Jackals will not forget their defeat. We must prepare for their return."

Murmurs of agreement rippled through the crowd, but Alaba felt their gazes shift toward him. He knew what was coming.

"Alaba," Pa Eze said, turning to face him. "You fought bravely, and for that, we are grateful. But we must ask: what will you do now?"

Alaba felt the weight of the question settle on his shoulders. He glanced at Adaeze, who stood at the edge of the crowd, her expression unreadable.

"I'll stay," he said finally, his voice steady. "I'll help rebuild. I'll train the men to fight, to defend themselves. If the Jackals come back, I'll be here."

A murmur spread through the crowd, some voices approving, others doubtful.

Pa Eze nodded slowly, though his expression remained guarded. "Very well," he said. "But know this: your past brought this trouble to our doorstep. If you stay, you must prove that you're more than the man you were. Actions, not words, will determine your place here."

—-

Over the next few days, Alaba threw himself into the work of rebuilding. He repaired fences, helped dig trenches, and led training sessions for the men. Slowly, the villagers began to warm to him, their initial skepticism tempered by his dedication.

Still, not everyone was convinced. Pa Eze watched Alaba closely, his gaze never lingering for long but always present. Chike, too, remained cautious, though he respected Alaba's skill and determination.

One afternoon, as Alaba was teaching a group of young men how to wield spears, Chike approached him.

"You're good at this," Chike said, nodding toward the group. "But I have to ask: why are you so determined to stay?"

Alaba paused, lowering his spear. He looked at Chike, his expression earnest.

"Because I have nowhere else to go," he admitted. "And because I owe this village. I owe Adaeze. She gave me a second chance when no one else would."

Chike studied him for a moment before nodding. "Just make sure you don't waste it."

—-

As the days turned into weeks, life in the village began to return to normal. The fields were tilled, the markets reopened, and the sound of laughter once again echoed through the streets.

But the threat of the Black Jackals loomed like a dark cloud. Every rustle in the trees, every distant shout, sent a ripple of fear through the villagers. Alaba could feel the tension, could see it in the way people glanced over their shoulders, their movements quick and guarded.

One evening, as the sun dipped below the horizon, Adaeze found Alaba sitting on a fallen log near the edge of the village. He was sharpening a machete, his face set in concentration.

"You've been quiet lately," she said, sitting beside him.

"There's a lot on my mind," he replied without looking up.

Adaeze hesitated before speaking again. "Do you think they'll come back?"

Alaba stopped sharpening the blade and looked at her. "Yes," he said simply. "It's only a matter of time."

Adaeze's expression faltered, but she quickly regained her composure. "Then we'll be ready," she said firmly.

Alaba gave her a small smile. "You're braver than most of the men here, you know that?"

"It's not bravery," she said. "It's necessity. If we don't fight for what we have, we'll lose it."

He nodded, his gaze drifting to the horizon. "You're right. But I just hope... I hope it's enough."

—-

That night, as the village slept, Alaba's thoughts kept him awake. He replayed the events of the past weeks in his mind, analyzing every decision, every mistake. He couldn't shake the feeling that he was still an outsider, that no matter what he did, he would always carry the shadow of his past.

His thoughts were interrupted by the sound of footsteps. He turned to see Adaeze approaching, a lantern in her hand.

"Can't sleep?" she asked, sitting beside him.

"No," he admitted. "There's too much to think about."

Adaeze looked at him, her expression soft. "You've done more for this village in a few weeks than most people have in years. You've earned your place here."

Alaba shook his head. "It's not just about earning a place. It's about making things right. And I don't know if I can ever do that."

"You can," she said firmly. "And you will. I believe in you, Alaba. So does this village, even if they don't all show it yet."

Her words settled over him like a warm blanket, soothing the ache in his chest. He looked at her, his gratitude shining in his eyes.

"Thank you," he said quietly.

They sat in silence for a while, the lantern casting a soft glow around them. In that moment, the weight of the world felt a little lighter.

But as Alaba looked toward the horizon, he couldn't shake the feeling that the storm was far from over. The Black Jackals would return, and when they did, they would bring chaos with them.

For now, though, he allowed himself a brief moment of peace, knowing that the fight for redemption—and survival—was far from finished.

8

A Storm on the Horizon

The village was alive with activity as preparations for the inevitable continued. Alaba had taken to patrolling the perimeter each morning, ensuring there were no breaches in the hastily erected defenses. He moved with purpose, his eyes scanning the forest for signs of danger.

The people of the village were growing stronger. Men who once flinched at the thought of holding a weapon now handled their spears with a practiced grip. Women who had hidden in their homes during the last attack now joined the efforts, gathering stones, sharpening blades, and fortifying weak spots in the village's defenses.

Alaba watched their transformation with a mix of pride and concern. These people were not warriors; they were farmers, traders, and artisans. Though their spirits were strong, he feared what another attack would mean for them.

—-

Later that day, as the sun reached its zenith, Pa Eze called for a council meeting in the village square. The elders gathered first, taking their seats on wooden benches shaded by a large mango tree. The rest of the villagers formed a loose circle around them, their faces solemn.

Pa Eze stood in the center, his cane in hand. His expression was grave as he addressed the crowd.

"Today, we must discuss the future of our village," he began, his voice heavy. "The Black Jackals will return. When they do, we must be prepared."

Murmurs spread through the crowd, a mixture of fear and determination.

"We've been working hard," Pa Eze continued, "but we cannot do this alone. We must seek allies."

"Who will help us?" an elder asked. "The neighboring villages are just as vulnerable as we are."

"There is one," Pa Eze replied, his gaze shifting to Alaba. "The warriors of Umunze. They are strong, and they owe us a debt from years past. But someone must go to them and convince them to join our cause."

All eyes turned to Alaba.

"I'll go," he said without hesitation.

Pa Eze nodded. "It will be dangerous. The Black Jackals may already be watching the roads. Are you certain?"

"I'm certain," Alaba replied. "If there's a chance they'll help, it's worth the risk."

—-

The next morning, Alaba set out at dawn. Adaeze met him at the edge of the village, holding a small pouch filled with food and water.

"Be careful," she said, her voice tinged with worry.

"I will," he promised, taking the pouch from her.

For a moment, they stood in silence, the weight of unspoken words hanging between them. Then, without thinking, Adaeze reached out and touched his arm.

"Come back to us," she said softly.

"I will," Alaba repeated, his voice firm.

With that, he turned and began his journey.

—-

The road to Umunze was long and fraught with danger. Alaba moved cautiously, his machete at the ready. The forest was alive with the sounds of rustling leaves, chirping birds, and the occasional snap of a branch. Each noise set his nerves on edge.

As the hours passed, the terrain grew rougher. The narrow path twisted through dense undergrowth, forcing Alaba to hack his way through at times. Sweat dripped from his brow, but he pressed on, driven by the knowledge that the village's survival depended on him.

It was near midday when he heard the first sign of trouble: the distant sound of voices.

Alaba froze, his hand tightening around his machete. The voices grew louder, accompanied by the crunch of boots on dry leaves. He crouched low, blending into the shadows of the trees.

A group of five men emerged from the undergrowth, their black-and-red clothing unmistakable. Black Jackals.

Alaba's heart raced as he watched them. They were laughing and talking, their weapons slung casually over their shoulders.

"We'll hit them again soon," one of them said. "This time, we'll leave nothing behind."

"Let them enjoy their little victory," another replied with a sneer. "It won't last."

Alaba's jaw tightened. He knew he couldn't take them all on alone, but he also couldn't risk letting them see him. He waited until they passed, their voices fading into the distance, before slipping away in the opposite direction.

By late afternoon, Alaba reached the outskirts of Umunze. The village was larger and more fortified than his own, with tall wooden walls and armed guards patrolling the perimeter.

He approached cautiously, his hands raised to show he meant no harm. The guards eyed him warily but allowed him inside after he explained his purpose.

Alaba was led to the village chief, a stern-looking man named Chief Ogbonna. The chief listened in silence as Alaba explained the situation, his expression unreadable.

"When the Black Jackals attacked us before, we asked for help," Chief Ogbonna said when Alaba finished. "Your people turned us away."

Alaba felt a pang of guilt, though the decision had been made long before his return. "I can't change the past," he said. "But I'm asking for your help now. If the Black Jackals aren't stopped, they'll come for you next."

Chief Ogbonna studied him for a long moment before nodding. "You're right. We'll help you. But on one condition: your village must send us half of this year's harvest as payment."

Alaba hesitated. The demand was steep, but he knew the village couldn't afford to refuse.

"Agreed," he said finally.

—-

As Alaba made his way back to the village that evening, his thoughts were heavy. He had secured the help of Umunze, but at a great cost. He only hoped the villagers would understand.

The journey back was uneventful, but Alaba's mind raced with plans. He thought about the defenses they would need to strengthen, the strategies they would need to devise.

When he finally arrived at the village, it was nearly midnight. Adaeze was waiting for him, her face lighting up with relief when she saw him.

"You're back," she said, her voice filled with emotion.

"I'm back," he replied, exhaustion evident in his tone.

"What did they say?" Pa Eze asked, stepping forward from the shadows.

"They'll help," Alaba said. "But they want half of our harvest in return."

The villagers murmured among themselves, their faces a mixture of relief and concern.

"It's a high price," Pa Eze said after a moment. "But if it means saving our village, it's worth it."

Alaba nodded, though he couldn't shake the feeling that the hardest part of their journey was yet to come. The storm was on the horizon, and it would test them all in ways they couldn't yet imagine.

9

Shadows of Betrayal

The first rays of dawn broke over the village, casting a golden glow on the carefully erected defenses. With the promise of Umunze's warriors bolstering their ranks, there was a renewed sense of hope among the villagers. But Alaba, standing on the edge of the village square, couldn't shake a lingering unease.

He'd done his part to secure allies, but the Black Jackals were cunning and ruthless. Their leader, a man known only as Ezenwa, was said to possess an uncanny ability to predict his enemies' moves. Alaba had faced many foes in his years away, but something about this man unnerved him.

As the day unfolded, the villagers continued their preparations. Training sessions were rigorous, and the rhythm of hammering and sharpening tools echoed through the air. Alaba took charge of leading the younger men and women in combat drills, teaching them techniques he had honed over the years.

But beneath the surface of this organized effort, whispers of doubt began to circulate. Some questioned the wisdom of giving up half of their harvest to Umunze, wondering if they could trust the larger village to honor their promise.

That evening, as the village gathered around a crackling fire for their nightly meeting, Pa Eze addressed the crowd.

"We stand at a crossroads," he began, his voice steady but tinged with weariness. "The help we've secured from Umunze comes at a cost, but it is necessary for our survival. Let us not forget that unity is our greatest weapon."

A murmur spread through the crowd. Most nodded in agreement, but a few faces were marked with skepticism.

Then, a man named Nkem, one of the more outspoken farmers, stepped forward. His tall, wiry frame cast a long shadow in the firelight.

"With all due respect, Pa Eze," he said, his voice loud enough for all to hear, "how can we be sure Umunze will come? What if they take our harvest and leave us to fend for ourselves?"

Gasps rippled through the crowd, and Pa Eze's eyes narrowed. Before he could respond, Alaba stepped forward.

"They will come," Alaba said firmly. "I spoke to their chief myself. He gave me his word."

"And we're supposed to trust the word of a man who wasn't here when we needed him?" Nkem retorted, his gaze locking with Alaba's. "You left us, Alaba. How do we know you're not leading us into another disaster?"

The tension in the air was palpable. Alaba felt the weight of the accusation but refused to waver.

"I left to protect my family," he said, his voice steady. "I've come back to protect all of you. I understand your fear, Nkem, but we don't have the luxury of division. If we don't trust each other, we've already lost."

Nkem hesitated, his expression softening slightly. But the seeds of doubt had been sown, and Alaba knew they would take root if left unchecked.

—-

Later that night, as the village settled into an uneasy quiet, Alaba found himself unable to sleep. He walked the perimeter of the village, his machete in hand, his eyes scanning the darkness for any signs of movement.

It was during one of these patrols that he overheard voices coming from the far edge of the village. Moving silently, he crept closer, his heart pounding in his chest.

"We can't keep following Pa Eze," one voice whispered. "This plan will get us all killed."

"It's risky," another voice replied, "but what choice do we have? If we stay, we're dead. If we leave, at least we have a chance."

Alaba's blood ran cold. He peered through the underbrush and saw a small group of villagers huddled together, their faces illuminated by the faint glow of a lantern.

Among them was Nkem.

"We'll leave tomorrow night," Nkem said. "Take our families and whatever supplies we can carry. Let the others fight this hopeless battle."

Alaba clenched his fists, anger and disappointment surging through him. He stepped into the clearing, his presence startling the group.

"Leaving won't save you," he said, his voice low but firm.

The group froze, their faces pale. Nkem was the first to recover, his jaw tightening as he glared at Alaba.

"And staying will?" Nkem shot back. "You're leading these people to their deaths, and you know it."

"I'm giving them a chance," Alaba replied. "Running will only make you easier targets. The Black Jackals don't leave survivors, Nkem. If you leave, you'll be hunted down before you even reach the next village."

For a moment, no one spoke. The weight of Alaba's words hung heavy in the air. Finally, one of the younger men in the group stepped forward.

"Is it true?" he asked, his voice trembling. "Will they hunt us if we run?"

"Yes," Alaba said. "They don't just want our village—they want to send a message. If we stand together, we have a chance. But divided, we're nothing."

The group exchanged uneasy glances, their resolve wavering.

"Think about your families," Alaba added. "The Black Jackals won't show them mercy. But if we fight, we can protect them."

Nkem's expression hardened, but he didn't argue further. Instead, he turned and walked away, leaving the clearing without another word. The others followed, their steps hesitant.

—-

The next morning, Alaba approached Pa Eze and told him what had happened. The elder sighed heavily, the weight of leadership etched into his features.

"People are afraid," Pa Eze said. "Fear makes them act rashly. But you've done well to confront them. Perhaps they'll see reason now."

Alaba nodded, though he couldn't shake the feeling that the village's unity was more fragile than ever.

—-

As the sun set that evening, Alaba called for a meeting of the village's fighters. Standing before them, he spoke with a mixture of urgency and determination.

"We cannot afford to falter," he said. "The Black Jackals will come, and when they do, they will show no mercy. But together, we are stronger than they realize. We have the support of Umunze, and we have the will to fight. That is enough."

The fighters nodded, their expressions a mixture of fear and resolve.

"We fight for our families, our home, and our future," Alaba continued. "Remember that when the time comes."

The group dispersed, their spirits bolstered by his words. But as Alaba stood alone under the darkening sky, he couldn't shake the feeling that betrayal still lurked in the shadows.

The storm was closer than ever, and Alaba knew they would need every ounce of strength and unity to weather it.

10

The Final Stand

The sun hung low in the sky, casting a blood-red hue over the village as the first distant sounds of drums reached the villagers' ears. The Black Jackals were coming. The moment of truth had arrived, and the air felt thick with tension. Alaba stood at the edge of the village, his eyes scanning the horizon, his mind racing through strategies, his thoughts swirling around his people's fate.

The warriors of Umunze had not yet arrived. Alaba knew that they might not come at all—after all, they had their own village to protect. But he had made a vow to the people of Umunze when he left their village years ago. He would protect the village that had taken him in, no matter the cost. The promise to his home village, the one he swore to uphold, kept him going.

He took one final look at the village, the women and children working together to fortify the homes, the fighters getting ready for the worst. Their faces were grim, and yet there was something else—something far more dangerous: hope. They hoped for a miracle, a hand to save them at the last moment. But deep down, Alaba knew hope alone would not be enough.

—-

As night descended and the village fell into a hushed silence, Alaba gathered his warriors. His eyes swept over their faces—men and women who had once been strangers to him, but now, they were his family. In them, he saw the same fear he had felt when he first left his village, the same uncertainty that came with every battle. But now, there was something different in their eyes—a glimmer of determination, a spark that mirrored his own.

"We stand together," Alaba began, his voice calm but resolute. "Tonight, we face the Black Jackals. They think we are weak, that they can easily crush us. But we will show them the strength of a people who fight for their home."

He paused, letting his words settle over the group.

"I've seen what they are capable of. They are ruthless, but they are not invincible. They have their weaknesses, and we know them. We are going to fight with everything we have—our strength, our wits, and our hearts. Together, we will push them back."

The warriors nodded, their faces hardening as they steeled themselves for the battle to come. Alaba's heart raced, but it was no longer with fear. It was with something far more powerful—resolve.

—-

The ground beneath them seemed to tremble as the Black Jackals finally arrived, their dark silhouettes moving through the dense trees like shadows in the night. There were dozens of them, their armor glinting in the moonlight, their weapons sharp and ready. Alaba could hear the clinking of chains and the faint murmur of their voices as they made their way toward the village, unaware of the trap that had been set.

With a signal from Alaba, the village's fighters moved into position, hiding behind trees, underbrush, and the walls they had hastily built. The air was thick with anticipation. Then, like the sharp crack of thunder, the battle began.

The Black Jackals charged forward, their leader, Ezenwa, at the front, his dark eyes scanning the village with calculated precision. He had underestimated the villagers. He had thought they were weak, easily subdued. But he was wrong.

Alaba's fighters emerged from their hiding places, ambushing the Black Jackals with swift, deadly precision. Arrows flew, catching several of the attackers off guard, while the villagers wielded their machetes and spears with surprising skill. The clash of steel echoed through the night, and the smell of sweat and blood filled the air.

But even as the villagers fought valiantly, it became clear that the Black Jackals were not an enemy to be taken lightly. They fought back with ferocity, each strike from Ezenwa and his warriors cutting through the villagers' ranks. The battle was fierce, a whirlwind of death and destruction, as the two sides fought tooth and nail for survival.

—-

Amid the chaos, Alaba found himself face-to-face with Ezenwa, the leader of the Black Jackals. The two men locked eyes, and in that moment, it was as if the world had paused. Alaba saw in Ezenwa's gaze the same ruthless determination that had driven him all those years ago when he first left the village in search of a better life. But now, there was something different—Ezenwa's eyes were filled with arrogance.

"You think you can stop us, Alaba?" Ezenwa sneered, raising his sword. "You are nothing. This village, these people—they are mine. You can't win."

Alaba gritted his teeth, his grip tightening on his machete. "This village will never belong to you, Ezenwa. Not while I breathe."

With a roar, Ezenwa lunged forward, his sword aimed straight for Alaba's chest. The force of the strike was immense, but Alaba managed to dodge, narrowly missing the blade. The two men circled each other, each waiting for the other to make a mistake.

Ezenwa was fast, his movements precise, but Alaba had something he didn't—years of experience. With a swift movement, Alaba ducked under Ezenwa's next strike and slashed his machete across the Black Jackal's side. Ezenwa hissed in pain but quickly recovered, anger flashing in his eyes.

"You're stronger than I thought," Ezenwa growled, wiping the blood from his face. "But it doesn't matter. You're still going to die."

With a furious yell, Ezenwa charged again. But this time, Alaba was ready. He sidestepped the attack, using Ezenwa's momentum against him. With a quick, decisive strike, Alaba drove his machete into Ezenwa's side, sinking it deep into the man's ribs.

Ezenwa staggered back, gasping for air as blood poured from the wound. His sword clattered to the ground, and his legs buckled beneath him.

"You... you should've stayed away," Ezenwa whispered, his eyes flickering with disbelief.

Alaba stood over him, his chest heaving, his machete slick with blood. "No," he said softly. "You should have."

With that, Ezenwa's body went limp, and the leader of the Black Jackals was no more.

—-

The battle raged on for what felt like hours, but with their leader fallen, the

Black Jackals began to falter. Alaba's warriors, emboldened by their victory over Ezenwa, pressed their advantage, pushing the remaining attackers back. Slowly but surely, the tide of the battle turned in their favor.

When the last of the Black Jackals were driven out of the village, the survivors stood amidst the carnage, breathing heavily, bloodied but victorious. The village was battered, but it had withstood the storm.

Alaba stood at the center of it all, his heart heavy with the loss of life, but also filled with a fierce pride. They had done it. They had fought for their home, and they had won.

He looked up at the stars, knowing that the battle was over—but the war for their survival would never truly end. But in that moment, surrounded by his people, Alaba knew one thing for sure: as long as they stood together, they could face anything.

The return of Alaba had brought them hope. And together, they would rebuild.

www.ingramcontent.com/pod-product-compliance
Lightning Source LLC
LaVergne TN
LVHW030345070526
838199LV00067B/6449